LET'S DO
BRUNCH

LET'S DO BRUNCH

PAVILION

First published in the United Kingdom in 2015 by
Pavilion
1 Gower Street
London
WC1E 6HD

The Good Housekeeping website is
www.goodhousekeeping.co.uk

ISBN 978-1-908449-95-5

A catalogue record for this book is available from
the British Library.

10 9 8 7 6 5 4

Reproduction by Dot Gradations Ltd, UK
Printed and bound by GPS, Slovenia

This book can be ordered direct from the publisher
at www.pavilionbooks.com

NOTES

Both metric and imperial measures are given for
the recipes. Follow either set of measures, not a
mixture of both, as they are not interchangeable.

All spoon measures are level.
1 tsp = 5ml spoon; 1 tbsp = 15ml spoon.

Ovens and grills must be preheated to the specified
temperature.

Medium eggs should be used except where
otherwise specified. Free-range eggs are
recommended.

Note that some recipes contain raw or lightly
cooked eggs. The young, elderly, pregnant women
and anyone with an immune-deficiency disease
should avoid these because of the slight risk of
salmonella.

Contents

Cereal and Fruit 6

Pastries and Muffins 32

Good Eggs 64

Sweet Plates 90

Sandwiches and Savouries 110

Smoothies and Drinks 134

Calorie Gallery 170

Index 174

Cereal and Fruit

Toasted Oats with Berries

Hands-on time: 10 minutes
Cooking time: about 10 minutes, plus cooling

25g (1oz) hazelnuts, roughly chopped
125g (4oz) rolled oats
1 tbsp olive oil
125g (4oz) strawberries, sliced
250g (9oz) blueberries
200g (7oz) Greek yogurt
2 tbsp runny honey

1 Preheat the grill to medium. Put the hazelnuts into a bowl with the oats. Drizzle with the oil and mix well, then spread out on a baking sheet. Toast the oat mixture for 5–10 minutes until it starts to crisp up. Remove from the heat and leave to cool.

2 Put the strawberries into a large bowl with the blueberries and yogurt. Stir in the oats and hazelnuts, drizzle with the honey and divide among four dishes. Serve immediately.

SAVE EFFORT

If you don't have any strawberries or blueberries to hand, substitute with other fruits, such as raspberries, blackberries and chopped nectarines or peaches.

Serves 4

Granola

Hands-on time: 5 minutes
Cooking time: 1 hour 5 minutes

300g (11oz) rolled oats

50g (2oz) each chopped Brazil nuts, flaked almonds, wheatgerm or rye flakes, and sunflower seeds

25g (1oz) sesame seeds

100ml (3½fl oz) sunflower oil

3 tbsp runny honey

100g (3½oz) each raisins and dried cranberries

milk or yogurt to serve

1 Preheat the oven to 140°C (120°C fan oven) mark 1. Put the oats, nuts, wheatgerm or rye flakes, and all the seeds into a bowl. Gently heat the oil and honey in a pan. Pour over the oats mixture and stir to combine. Spread on a shallow baking tray and bake in the oven for 1 hour or until golden, stirring once. Leave to cool.

2 Transfer to a large bowl and stir in the raisins and dried cranberries. Store in an airtight container – the granola will keep for up to a week. Serve with milk or yogurt.

HEALTHY TIP

Granola is an excellent breakfast option because the oats provide a sustained rise in blood sugar, helping to keep hunger at bay longer. Brazil nuts used in this recipe are rich in selenium, a powerful antioxidant nutrient, while the almonds supply valuable amounts of bone-building calcium, protein and zinc.

Makes 15 servings

Porridge with Dried Fruit

Hands-on time: 5 minutes
Cooking time: 5 minutes

200g (7oz) porridge oats

400ml (14fl oz) milk, plus extra
to serve

75g (3oz) mixture of chopped dried figs,
apricots and raisins

1 Put the oats into a large pan and add the milk and 400ml (14fl oz) water. Stir in the figs, apricots and raisins and heat gently, stirring until the porridge thickens and the oats are cooked.

2 Divide among four bowls and serve with a splash of milk.

Muesli bars

Some of the simplest biscuits to make are traybakes, which are cooked in one piece and then cut into bars. The mixtures often contain fruit, nuts and oats.

To make 12 bars, you will need:
175g (6oz) unsalted butter, cut into pieces, 150g (5oz) light muscovado sugar, 2 tbsp golden syrup, 375g (13oz) porridge oats, 100g (3½oz) ready-to-eat dried papaya, roughly chopped, 50g (2oz) sultanas, 50g (2oz) pecan nuts, roughly chopped, 25g (1oz) pinenuts, 25g (1oz) pumpkin seeds, 1 tbsp plain flour and 1 tsp ground cinnamon.

1 Preheat the oven to 180°C (160°C fan oven) mark 4. Melt the butter, sugar and golden syrup together in a heavy-based pan over a low heat.

2 Meanwhile, put the oats, dried fruit, nuts, seeds, flour and cinnamon into a large bowl and stir to mix. Pour in the melted mixture and mix together until combined.

3 Spoon the mixture into a 30.5 × 20.5cm (12 × 8in) non-stick baking tin and press down into the corners.

4 Bake for 25–30 minutes or until golden. Press the mixture down again if necessary, then use a palette knife to mark into 12 bars.

5 Leave to cool completely. Use a palette knife to lift the bars out of the tin and store them in an airtight container.

FREEZE AHEAD

Store individually wrapped muesli bars in the freezer. Remove and defrost for a couple of hours for the perfect mid-morning snack.

Energy-boosting Muesli

Hands-on time: 5 minutes

500g (1lb 2oz) porridge oats

100g (3½oz) toasted almonds, chopped

2 tbsp pumpkin seeds

2 tbsp sunflower seeds

100g (3½oz) ready-to-eat dried apricots,
   chopped

milk or yogurt to serve

1 Mix the oats with the almonds, seeds
   and apricots. Store in a sealable
   container: it will keep for up to one
   month. Serve with milk or yogurt.

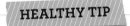

HEALTHY TIP

Dried apricots are a rich source
of fibre and iron, as well as
vitamins A and C.

Makes 15 servings

Apple and Almond Yogurt

500g (1lb 2oz) natural yogurt

50g (2oz) each sultanas and
flaked almonds

2 apples

1 Put the yogurt into a bowl and add the sultanas and almonds.

2 Grate the apples, add to the bowl and mix together. Chill in the fridge overnight. Use as a topping for breakfast cereal or serve as a snack.

SAVE EFFORT

If you don't have any apples, you could use pears instead. You can also replace the sultanas with dried cranberries.

Serves 4

Breakfast Bruschetta

Hands-on time: 5 minutes
Cooking time: 5 minutes

1 ripe banana, peeled and sliced
250g (9oz) blueberries
200g (7oz) quark cheese
4 slices pumpernickel or wheat-free
   wholegrain bread
1 tbsp runny honey

1 Put the banana into a bowl with
  the blueberries. Spoon in the quark
  cheese and mix well.
2 Toast the slices of bread on both
  sides, then spread with the blueberry
  mixture. Drizzle with honey and
  serve immediately.

HEALTHY TIP

This toasted treat is very low in fat.
Pumpernickel bread is made from
rye flour, which is rich in fibre,
iron and zinc. The blueberries are
rich in anthocyanins, which help
combat heart disease, certain
cancers and strokes.

Serves 4

Apple Compote

Hands-on time: 10 minutes, plus chilling
Cooking time: 5 minutes, plus cooling

250g (9oz) cooking apples, peeled
and chopped

juice of ½ lemon

1 tbsp golden caster sugar

ground cinnamon

25g (1oz) raisins; 25g (1oz) chopped
almonds; 1 tbsp natural yogurt
to serve

1 Put the cooking apples into a pan
with the lemon juice, caster sugar
and 2 tbsp cold water. Cook gently
for 5 minutes or until soft. Transfer
to a bowl.

2 Sprinkle a little ground cinnamon
over the top, cool and chill. It will
keep for up to three days.

3 Serve with the raisins, chopped
almonds and yogurt.

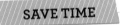

SAVE TIME

To microwave, put the apples,
lemon juice, sugar and water into a
microwave-proof bowl, cover loosely
with clingfilm and microwave on
full power (850W) for 4 minutes or
until the apples are just soft.

Serves 2

Perfect Berries

Soft fruits – strawberries, blackberries, raspberries and currants –
are generally quick to prepare. Always handle ripe fruits gently
as they can be delicate.

Washing berries

Most soft fruits can be washed very
gently in cold water. Shop-bought
blackberries will usually have the
hull removed. If you have picked
blackberries yourself the hulls and
stalks may still be attached, so pick
over the berries carefully and remove
any that remain. Raspberries are very
delicate, so handle very carefully;
remove any stalks and hulls. Leave
strawberries whole.

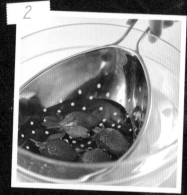

1 Place the berries in a bowl of cold
   water and allow any small pieces
   of grit, dust or insects to float out.
2 Transfer the fruit to a colander
   and rinse gently under fresh
   running water. Drain well, then
   leave to drain on kitchen paper.

Hulling strawberries

1 Wash the strawberries gently and dry on kitchen paper. Remove the hull (the centre part that was attached to the plant) from the strawberry using a strawberry huller or a small sharp knife.

2 Put the knife into the small, hard area beneath the green stalk and gently rotate to remove a small, cone-shaped piece.

Strawberry Compote

Hands-on time: 15 minutes, plus overnight chilling
Cooking time: 10 minutes, plus cooling

175g (6oz) raspberry conserve

juice of 1 orange

juice of 1 lemon

1 tsp rose water

350g (12oz) strawberries, hulled and thickly sliced

150g (5oz) blueberries

1 Put the raspberry conserve into a pan with the orange and lemon juices and add 75ml (2½fl oz) boiling water. Stir over a low heat to dissolve the conserve, then leave to cool.

2 Stir in the rose water and taste – you may want to add a squeeze more lemon juice if it's too sweet. Put the strawberries and blueberries into a large serving bowl, then strain the raspberry conserve mixture over them. Cover and chill overnight. Remove the bowl from the fridge 30 minutes before serving.

HEALTHY TIP

Berries are densely packed with vitamins, antioxidants and other phytonutrients (highly nutritious, active compounds found within fruits, vegetables, whole grains, beans, pulses, nuts and seeds, and herbs and spices). Berries also contain compounds called anthocyanins – the pigment that gives berries their intense colour, mops up damaging free radicals and helps prevent cancer and heart disease. Combined with vitamin C, anthocyanins help to improve blood flow around the body.

Serves 4

Exotic Fruit Salad

Hands-on time: 10 minutes

2 oranges, cut into segments

1 mango, peeled, stoned and chopped (see page 156)

450g (1lb) peeled and diced fresh pineapple (see page 157)

200g (7oz) blueberries

½ Charentais melon, cubed

grated zest and juice of 1 lime

1 Put the orange segments into a bowl and add the mango, pineapple, blueberries and melon. Add the lime zest and juice.

2 Gently mix the fruit together and serve immediately.

HEALTHY TIP

Fresh pineapple contains the enzyme bromelain, which aids digestion and is beneficial for inflammatory conditions such as sinusitis and rheumatoid arthritis.

Serves 4

Tropical Fruit Pots

Hands-on time: 15 minutes
Cooking time: 5 minutes

400g can apricots in fruit juice

2 balls of preserved stem ginger
in syrup, finely chopped, plus
2 tbsp syrup from the jar

½ tsp ground cinnamon

juice of 1 orange

3 oranges, cut into segments

1 mango, peeled, stoned and chopped
(see page 156)

1 pineapple, peeled, core removed,
and chopped (see page 157)

450g (1lb) coconut yogurt

3 tbsp lemon curd

3–4 tbsp light muscovado sugar

1 Drain the juice from the apricots into
a pan and stir in the syrup from the
ginger. Add the chopped stem ginger,
the cinnamon and orange juice. Put
over a low heat and stir gently. Bring
to the boil, then reduce the heat and
simmer for 2–3 minutes to make a
thick syrup.

2 Roughly chop the apricots and put
into a bowl with the segmented
oranges, the mango and pineapple.
Pour the syrup over the fruit. Divide
among eight 300ml (½ pint) glasses
or dessert bowls.

3 Beat the yogurt and lemon curd
together in a bowl until smooth.
Spoon a generous dollop over the fruit
and sprinkle with muscovado sugar.
Chill if not serving immediately.

SAVE TIME

To prepare ahead complete the
recipe to the end of step 2 up to
2 hours before you plan to eat –
no need to chill.

Serves 8

Pastries
and Muffins

Croissants

Hands-on time: 40 minutes, plus chilling and standing
Cooking time: 15 minutes

25g (1oz) fresh yeast or 1 tbsp dried yeast
and 1 tsp sugar

2 medium eggs

450g (1lb) strong white flour, plus extra
to dust

2 tsp salt

25g (1oz) lard

225g (8oz) unsalted butter, at cool room
temperature

½ tsp caster sugar

1 Blend the fresh yeast with 225ml
(8fl oz) tepid water. If using dried
yeast, sprinkle it into the water with
the 1 tsp sugar and leave in a warm
place for 15 minutes or until frothy.

2 Whisk 1 egg into the yeast liquid. Sift
the flour and salt into a large bowl
and rub in the lard. Make a well in the
centre and pour in the yeast liquid.
Mix and then beat in the flour until
the bowl is left clean. Turn out on to a
lightly floured worksurface and knead
well for about 10 minutes until the
dough is firm and elastic.

3 Roll out the dough on a lightly floured
worksurface to an oblong about 51 ×
20.5cm (20 × 8in). Keep the edges as
square as possible, gently pulling out
the corners to stop them rounding
off. Dust the rolling pin with flour to
prevent it sticking to the dough.

4 Divide the butter into three. Dot one
portion over the top two-thirds of
the dough but clear of the edge. Turn
up the bottom third of the dough
over half the butter, then fold down
the remainder. Seal the edges with a
rolling pin. Turn the dough so that the
fold is on the right.

5 Press the dough lightly at intervals
along its length, then roll out to an
oblong again. Repeat the rolling and
folding with the other two portions of
butter. Rest the dough in the fridge
for 30 minutes, loosely covered with
a clean teatowel. Repeat three more
times, cover and chill for 1 hour.

6 Roll out the dough to an oblong about
48 × 33cm (19 × 13in), lay a clean

teatowel over the top and leave to rest for 10 minutes. Trim off 1cm (½in) all around and divide the dough in half lengthways, then into three squares, then across into triangles.

7 Beat the remaining egg, 1 tbsp water and the sugar together for the glaze and brush it over the triangles. Roll each triangle up from the long edge, finishing with the tip underneath. Curve into crescents and place well apart on ungreased baking sheets, allowing room to spread. Cover loosely with a clean teatowel. Leave at room temperature for about 30 minutes until well risen and 'puffy'.

8 Preheat the oven to 220°C (200°C fan oven) mark 7. Brush each croissant carefully with more glaze. Bake for 15 minutes or until crisp and well browned.

Croissants (see previous page)

Makes 12

Danish Pastries (see overleaf)

Makes 16

Danish Pastries

Hands-on time: 1 hour, plus rising and resting
Cooking time: 15 minutes

25g (1oz) fresh yeast or 1 tbsp dried yeast
  and 1 tsp sugar

450g (1lb) plain white flour, plus extra
  to dust

1 tsp salt

50g (2oz) lard

2 tbsp sugar

2 medium eggs, beaten

275g (10oz) butter, softened

1 medium egg, beaten, to glaze

glacé icing and flaked almonds,
  to decorate

For the almond paste

15g (½oz) butter

75g (3oz) caster sugar

75g (3oz) ground almonds

1 medium egg, beaten

For the cinnamon butter

50g (2oz) butter

50g (2oz) caster sugar

2 tsp ground cinnamon

1 Blend the fresh yeast with 150ml (¼ pint) tepid water. If using dried yeast, sprinkle it into the water with the 1 tsp sugar and leave in a warm place for 15 minutes or until frothy.

2 Mix the flour and salt, rub in the lard and stir in the 2 tbsp sugar. Add the yeast liquid and beaten eggs and mix to an elastic dough, adding a little more water if necessary. Knead well for 5 minutes on a lightly floured worksurface until smooth. Put the dough back into the rinsed-out bowl, cover with a clean teatowel and leave to rest in the fridge for 10 minutes.

3 Shape the butter into a rectangle. Roll out the dough on a floured board to a rectangle about three times as wide as the butter. Put the butter in the centre of the dough and fold the sides of the dough over the butter. Press the edges to seal.

4 With the folds at the sides, roll the dough into a strip three times as long as it is wide; fold the bottom third up,

and the top third down, cover and rest for 10 minutes. Turn and repeat the rolling, folding and resting twice more.

5 To make the almond paste, cream the butter and sugar, stir in the almonds and add enough egg to make a soft and pliable consistency. Make the cinnamon butter by creaming the butter and sugar and beating in the cinnamon.

6 Roll out the dough into the required shapes (see below) and fill with almond paste or cinnamon butter. Cover the pastries with a clean teatowel and leave in a warm place for 20–30 minutes until doubled in size. Preheat the oven to 220°C (200°C fan oven) mark 7.

7 Brush the pastries with beaten egg. Bake for 15 minutes or until golden. While hot, brush the pastries with thin glacé icing and sprinkle with flaked almonds.

To shape the pastries

Imperial stars Cut into 7.5cm (3in) squares. Make diagonal cuts from each corner to within 1cm (½in) of the centre. Put a piece of almond paste in the centre. Fold one corner of each cut section down to the centre, secure the tips with beaten egg.

Foldovers and cushions Cut into 7.5cm (3in) squares and put a little almond paste in the centre. Fold over two opposite corners to the centre. Make a cushion by folding over all four corners, securing the tips with beaten egg.

Twists Cut into 25.5 × 10cm (10 × 4in) rectangles. Cut each rectangle lengthways to give four pieces. Spread with cinnamon butter and fold the bottom third of each up and the top third down; seal and cut each across into thin slices. Form into twists.

Crumpets

Hands-on time: 20 minutes, plus rising
Cooking time: about 35 minutes

350g (12oz) strong plain white flour

½ tsp salt

½ tsp bicarbonate of soda

1½ tsp fast-action dried yeast

250ml (9fl oz) warm milk

a little vegetable oil to fry

butter to serve

1 Sift the flour, salt and bicarbonate of soda into a large bowl and stir in the yeast. Make a well in the centre, then pour in 300ml (½ pint) warm water and the warm milk. Mix to a thick batter.

2 Using a wooden spoon, beat the batter vigorously for about 5 minutes. Cover and leave in a warm place for about 1 hour until sponge-like in texture. Beat the batter for a further 2 minutes, then transfer to a jug.

3 Put a large, non-stick frying pan over a high heat and brush a little oil over the surface. Oil the insides of four crumpet rings or 7.5cm (3in) plain metal cutters. Put the rings, blunt-edge down, on the hot pan's surface and leave for about 2 minutes until very hot.

4 Pour a little batter into each ring to a depth of 1cm (½in). Cook the crumpets for 4–5 minutes until the surface is set and appears honeycombed with holes.

5 Carefully remove each metal ring. Flip the crumpets over and cook the other side for 1 minute only. Transfer to a wire rack. Repeat to use all of the batter.

6 To serve, toast the crumpets on both sides and serve with butter.

Makes about 24

Oven Scones

Hands-on time: 15 minutes
Cooking time: 10 minutes, plus cooling

40g (1½oz) butter, diced, plus extra
   to grease

225g (8oz) self-raising flour, plus extra
   to dust

a pinch of salt

1 tsp baking powder

about 150ml (¼ pint) milk

beaten egg or milk to glaze

whipped cream, or butter and jam
   to serve

SAVE EFFORT

To ensure a good rise, avoid heavy handling and make sure the rolled-out dough is at least 2cm (¾in) thick.

1 Preheat the oven to 220°C (200°C fan oven) mark 7. Grease a baking sheet. Sift the flour, salt and baking powder into a bowl. Rub in the butter until the mixture resembles fine breadcrumbs. Using a knife to stir it in, add enough milk to give a fairly soft dough.

2 Gently roll or pat out the dough on a lightly floured worksurface to a 2cm (¾in) thickness and then, using a 6cm (2½in) plain cutter, cut out rounds.

3 Put on the baking sheet and brush the tops with beaten egg or milk. Bake for about 10 minutes until golden brown and well risen. Transfer to a wire rack and leave to cool.

4 Serve warm, split and filled with cream, or butter and jam.

Makes 8

Cinnamon Whirls

Hands-on time: 20 minutes
Cooking time: 20 minutes, plus cooling

3 tbsp golden caster sugar, plus extra to dust

375g ready-rolled puff pastry

1 tsp ground cinnamon

1 tsp ground mixed spice

1 medium egg, beaten

1 Preheat the oven to 200°C (180°C fan oven) mark 6. Sprinkle the worksurface with caster sugar in a rectangle measuring 35.5 × 23cm (14 × 9in). Unroll the pastry and lay it on top to fit the shape of the sugar rectangle. Trim the edges, then cut vertically down the middle to make two smaller rectangles.

2 Mix the cinnamon with the mixed spice and remaining sugar in a small bowl. Sprinkle half the spice mixture evenly over the pastry rectangles. Fold the top and bottom edges of the pastry pieces into the middle so they meet at the centre. Sprinkle the remaining spice mixture over the surface and repeat, folding the upper and lower folded edges in to meet in the centre. Finally, fold in half lengthways to make a log shape.

3 Turn each roll over so that the seam faces down, trim off the ragged ends, then cut into slices 1cm (½in) wide. Lay the slices flat, spaced well apart, on two non-stick baking sheets. Reshape them slightly if needed, but don't worry if the rolls look loose – as the pastry cooks, they'll puff up.

4 Lightly brush each pastry whirl with a little beaten egg, sprinkle with a dusting of sugar and bake for 20 minutes or until pale golden. Transfer to a wire rack and leave to cool before serving.

Basic Baking Equipment

A selection of basic equipment is compulsory in order to bake successfully. Start with a few basic items and add to your collection as your skills increase (and as the demands of the recipe dictate).

Scales

Accurate measurement is essential when following most baking recipes. The electronic scale is the most accurate and can weigh up to 2kg (4½lb) or 5kg (11lb) in increments of 1–5g. Buy one with a flat platform on which you can put your bowl or measuring jug. Always set the scale to zero before adding the ingredients.

Measuring jugs, cups and spoons

Jugs can be plastic or glass, and are available, marked with both metric and imperial, in sizes ranging from 500ml (17fl oz) to 2 litres (3½ pints), or even 3 litres (5¼ pints). Measuring cups are bought in sets of ¼, ⅓, ½ and 1 cups. A standard 1 cup measure is equivalent to about 250ml (9fl oz). Measuring spoons are useful for the smallest units and accurate spoon measurements go up to 15ml (1 tbsp).

These may be in plastic or metal and often come in sets attached together on a ring.

Mixing bowls

Stainless steel bowls work best when you are using a hand-held whisk, or when you need to place the bowl into a larger bowl filled with iced water for chilling down or to place it over simmering water (when melting chocolate, for example). Plastic or glass bowls are best if you need to use them in the microwave. Bowls with gently tapered sides – much wider at the rim than at the base – will be useful for mixing dough.

Mixing spoons

For general mixing, the cheap and sturdy wooden spoon still can't be beaten. The spoon should be stiff, so that it can cope with thick mixtures such as dough. In addition, a large metal spoon for folding ingredients together is an invaluable item to have.

Bakeware

As well as being thin enough to conduct heat quickly and efficiently, bakeware should be sturdy enough not to warp. Most bakeware is made from aluminium, and it may have enamel or non-stick coatings. A newer material for some bakeware is flexible, oven-safe silicone.

It is safe to touch straight from the oven, is inherently non-stick and is also flexible – making it a lot easier to remove muffins and other bakes from their pans than it used to be.

Baking trays/Baking sheets

Shallower than a roasting tin, these have many uses in baking. To avoid having to bake in batches, choose ones that are large (but which fit comfortably in your oven). Buy the best you can afford.

Baking dishes

Are usually ceramic or Pyrex and you should have them in several sizes, ranging from 15–23cm (6–9in) to 25.5–35.5cm (10–14in).

Cake tins

Available in many shapes and sizes, tins may be single-piece, loose-based or springform.

Loaf tins

Available in various sizes, but one of the most useful is a 900g (2lb) tin.

Pie tins

You should have both single-piece tins and loose-based tins for flans and pies.

Muffin tins

These come in various sizes and depths and are available in both aluminium and silicone. If you make a lot of muffins and cupcakes it's worth investing in different types.

Honey and Spice Loaf Cake

Hands-on time: 20 minutes
Cooking time: about 55 minutes, plus cooling and setting

2 tbsp runny honey

200g (7oz) unsalted butter

80g (3¼oz) dark soft brown sugar

2 large eggs

200g (7oz) self-raising flour

1½ tsp mixed spice

100g (3½oz) icing sugar, sifted

butter to serve (optional)

1 Put the honey, butter and brown sugar into a pan and melt together over a low heat. When the sugar has dissolved, turn up the heat and leave to bubble for 1 minute. Take off the heat and leave to cool for 15 minutes.

2 Preheat the oven to 160°C (140°C fan oven) mark 3. Line a 900g (2lb) loaf tin with baking parchment.

3 Mix the eggs into the melted butter. Sift the flour and mixed spice into a large bowl and add the butter mixture. Mix well, then pour into the prepared tin.

4 Bake for 40–50 minutes until a skewer inserted into the centre comes out clean. Leave to cool in the tin for 5 minutes, then turn out on to a wire rack (leave the lining paper on) and leave to cool completely. When the cake is cold, peel off the lining paper and put the cake on a serving plate.

5 To make the glaze, put the icing sugar into a bowl and whisk in just enough water to get a runny consistency. Drizzle over the cake and leave to harden a little. Serve in slices, spread with butter if you like.

Cuts into 8 slices

Perfect Muffins

Muffins and cupcakes are two members of the same family: individual cakes, usually based on a mixture made with self-raising flour, baked in bun tins or muffin pans so that it rises and sets to an airy texture.

Banana and pecan muffins

To make 12 muffins, you will need: 275g (10oz) self-raising flour, 1 tsp bicarbonate of soda, a pinch of salt, 3 very ripe large bananas, about 450g (1lb), peeled and mashed, 125g (4oz) golden caster sugar, 1 large egg, 50ml (2fl oz) milk, 75g (3oz) melted butter and 50g (2oz) chopped roasted pecan nuts.

1 Preheat the oven to 180°C (160°C fan oven) mark 4. Line a 12-hole muffin tin with paper muffin cases. Sift together the flour, bicarbonate of soda and salt and put to one side.

2 Combine the bananas, sugar, egg and milk, then pour in the melted butter and mix well. Add to the flour mixture with the nuts, stirring quickly and gently with just a few strokes. Half-fill the muffin cases.

3 Bake for 20 minutes or until golden and risen. Transfer to a wire rack and leave to cool.

SAVE EFFORT

The secret to really light, fluffy muffins is a light hand, so be sure to sift the flour. Stir the mixture as little as possible; it's okay if it looks a little lumpy. Over-mixing will give tough, chewy results.

Cheesy Spinach Muffins

Hands-on time: 15 minutes
Cooking time: 12–15 minutes

100g (3½oz) baby spinach

150g (5oz) self-raising flour

1 tsp baking powder

25g (1oz) vegetarian Parmesan-style cheese, grated

50g (2oz) vegetarian Cheddar, finely cubed

25g (1oz) butter, melted

100ml (3½fl oz) milk

2 medium eggs

a small handful of fresh parsley, finely chopped

salt and ground black pepper

1 Preheat the oven to 200°C (180°C fan oven) mark 6. Line six holes in a 12-hole muffin tin with paper muffin cases. Put the spinach into a sieve and pour over boiling water from the kettle until it wilts. Leave the spinach to cool, then squeeze out as much water as you can before finely chopping it. Put to one side.

2 In a large bowl, mix together the flour, baking powder, most of the Parmesan and Cheddar cheeses and some seasoning.

3 In a separate jug, whisk together the butter, milk, eggs, parsley and chopped spinach. Quickly mix the wet ingredients into the dry. Don't worry if there are floury lumps, as these will cook out.

4 Divide the mixture evenly among the paper cases, then sprinkle over the remaining cheese. Cook for 12–15 minutes until the muffins are risen, golden and cooked through. Serve warm.

SAVE TIME

Prepare the muffins to the end of step 2 up to one day in advance. Put the chopped spinach into a bowl, then cover and chill. Cover the flour and cheese mixture and chill, then complete the recipe to serve.

Makes 6

Honey and Yogurt Muffins

Hands-on time: 15 minutes
Cooking time: about 20 minutes, plus cooling

225g (8oz) plain flour

1½ tsp baking powder

1 tsp bicarbonate of soda

½ tsp each ground mixed spice and ground nutmeg

pinch of salt

50g (2oz) ground oatmeal

50g (2oz) light muscovado sugar

225g (8oz) Greek-style yogurt

125ml (4fl oz) milk

1 medium egg

50g (2oz) butter, melted and cooled

4 tbsp runny honey

1 Preheat the oven to 200°C (180°C fan oven) mark 6. Line a 12-hole bun tin or muffin tin with paper muffin cases.
2 Sift the flour, baking powder, bicarbonate of soda, mixed spice, nutmeg and salt into a bowl. Stir in the oatmeal and sugar.
3 Mix the yogurt with the milk in a bowl, then beat in the egg, butter and honey. Pour on to the dry ingredients and stir in until just blended – don't overmix. Divide the mixture between the paper cases.
4 Bake for 17–20 minutes until the muffins are well risen and just firm. Cool in the tin for 5 minutes, then transfer to a wire rack. Serve warm or cold. These are best eaten on the day they are made.

FREEZE AHEAD

To freeze ahead, complete the recipe, cool then pack, seal and freeze. Thaw at room temperate when ready to use.

Bran and Apple Muffins

Hands-on time: 20 minutes
Cooking time: 30 minutes, plus cooling

250ml (9fl oz) semi-skimmed milk

2 tbsp orange juice

50g (2oz) All Bran

9 ready-to-eat dried prunes

100g (3½oz) light muscovado sugar

2 medium egg whites

1 tbsp golden syrup

150g (5oz) plain flour, sifted

1 tsp baking powder

1 tsp ground cinnamon

1 eating apple, peeled and grated

demerara sugar to sprinkle

1 Preheat the oven to 190°C (170°C fan oven) mark 5. Line a bun tin or muffin tin with 10 paper muffin cases.

2 Mix the milk and orange juice with the All Bran in a bowl. Put to one side for 10 minutes.

3 Put the prunes into a food processor or blender with 100ml (3½fl oz) water and whiz for 2–3 minutes to make a purée, then add the muscovado sugar and whiz briefly to mix.

4 Put the egg whites into a clean, grease-free bowl and whisk until soft peaks form. Add the whites to the milk mixture with the golden syrup, flour, baking powder, cinnamon, grated apple and prune mixture. Fold all the ingredients together gently – don't over-mix or the muffins will be tough.

5 Spoon the mixture into the paper cases and bake for 30 minutes or until well risen and golden brown. Cool on a wire rack. Sprinkle with demerara sugar just before serving. Best eaten on the day they are made.

Makes 10

Blueberry Muffins

Hands-on time: 10 minutes
Cooking time: about 25 minutes, plus cooling

2 medium eggs

250ml (9fl oz) semi-skimmed milk

250g (9oz) golden granulated sugar

2 tsp vanilla extract

350g (12oz) plain flour

4 tsp baking powder

250g (9oz) blueberries, frozen

finely grated zest of 2 lemons

HEALTHY TIP

Blueberries are bursting with health-boosting nutrients; they're rich in antioxidants, minerals and vitamins A, B, C and E.

1 Preheat the oven to 200°C (180°C fan oven) mark 6. Line a 12-hole muffin tin with paper muffin cases.

2 Put the eggs, milk, sugar and vanilla extract into a bowl and mix well.

3 Sift the flour and baking powder together into another bowl, then add the blueberries and lemon zest. Toss together and make a well in the centre.

4 Pour the egg mixture into the flour and blueberries and mix in gently – over-beating will make the muffins tough. Spoon the mixture equally into the paper cases.

5 Bake for 20–25 minutes until risen and just firm. Transfer to a wire rack and leave to cool completely. These are best eaten on the day they are made.

Makes 12

Spiced Carrot Muffins

Hands-on time: 30 minutes
Cooking time: about 25 minutes, plus cooling

125g (4oz) unsalted butter, softened

125g (4oz) light muscovado sugar

3 pieces preserved stem ginger, drained and chopped

150g (5oz) self-raising flour, sifted

1½ tsp baking powder

1 tbsp ground mixed spice

25g (1oz) ground almonds

3 medium eggs

finely grated zest of ½ orange

150g (5oz) carrots, peeled and grated

50g (2oz) pecan nuts, chopped

50g (2oz) sultanas

For the topping and decoration

200g (7oz) cream cheese

75g (3oz) icing sugar

1 tsp lemon juice

3 tbsp white rum or orange liqueur (optional)

12 unsprayed rose petals (optional)

1 Preheat the oven to 180°C (160°C fan oven) mark 4. Line a 12-hole muffin tin with paper muffin cases.

2 Beat the butter, muscovado sugar and stem ginger together until pale and creamy. Add the flour, baking powder, spice, ground almonds, eggs and orange zest and beat well until combined. Stir in the carrots, pecan nuts and sultanas. Spoon the mixture equally into the paper cases.

3 Bake for 20–25 minutes until risen and just firm. A skewer inserted into the centre of a cupcake should come out clean. Transfer to a wire rack and leave to cool completely.

4 To make the topping, beat the cream cheese in a bowl until softened. Beat in the icing sugar and lemon juice to give a smooth icing that just holds its shape.

Makes 12

5 Drizzle each cake with a little liqueur,
  if you like. Using a small palette knife,
  spread a little icing over each cake.
  Decorate with a rose petal, if you like.

HEALTHY TIP

Carrots are an excellent source of
vitamin A, while pecan nuts are a
rich source of vitamin E.

Brown Sugar Muffins

Hands-on time: 10 minutes
Cooking time: about 35 minutes, plus cooling

12 brown sugar cubes
150g (5oz) plain flour
1½ tsp baking powder
¼ tsp salt
1 medium egg, beaten
40g (1½oz) golden caster sugar
50g (2oz) unsalted butter, melted
½ tsp vanilla extract
100ml (3½fl oz) milk

1 Preheat the oven to 200°C (180°C fan oven) mark 6. Line a bun tin or muffin tin with six paper muffin cases.

2 Roughly crush the sugar cubes and put to one side. Sift together the flour, baking powder and salt.

3 In a large bowl, combine the beaten egg, caster sugar, melted butter, vanilla extract and milk.

4 Fold in the sifted flour and spoon the mixture into the paper cases. Sprinkle with the brown sugar.
Bake for 30–35 minutes. Leave to cool on a wire rack.

SAVE EFFORT

Quickly transform this recipe into apple and cinnamon muffins, fold 5 tbsp ready-made chunky apple sauce and 1 tsp ground cinnamon into the mixture with the flour.

Makes 6

Good Eggs

Classic Omelette

Hands-on time: 5 minutes
Cooking time: 5 minutes

2–3 medium eggs

1 tbsp milk or water

25g (1oz) unsalted butter

salt and freshly ground black pepper

sliced or grilled tomatoes and freshly
    chopped flat-leafed parsley to serve

1 Whisk the eggs in a bowl, just enough
to break them down – over-beating
spoils the texture of the omelette.
Season and add the milk or water.

2 Heat the butter in an 18cm (7in)
omelette pan or non-stick frying pan
until it is foaming, but not brown. Add
the eggs and stir gently with a fork or
wooden spatula, drawing the mixture
from the sides to the centre as it sets
and letting the liquid egg in the centre
run to the sides. When set, stop stirring
and cook for 30 seconds or until the
omelette is golden brown underneath
and still creamy on top: don't overcook.
If you are making a filled omelette, add
the filling at this point.

3 Tilt the pan away from you slightly
and use a palette knife to fold over
one-third of the omelette to the centre,
then fold over the opposite third.
Slide the omelette out on to a warmed
plate, letting it flip over so that the
folded sides are underneath. Serve
immediately, with tomatoes sprinkled
with parsley.

HEALTHY TIP

Eggs are a good protein source, with
one egg providing about one-sixth
of our daily requirement.

Omelette Arnold Bennett

Hands-on time: 15 minutes
Cooking time: about 20 minutes

125g (4oz) smoked haddock

50g (2oz) butter

150ml (¼ pint) double or single cream

3 medium eggs, separated

50g (2oz) Cheddar, grated

salt and freshly ground black pepper

rocket salad to serve

1 Put the fish in a pan and cover with water. Bring to the boil, reduce the heat and simmer gently for 10 minutes. Drain and flake the fish, discarding the skin and bones.

2 Put the fish in a pan with half the butter and 2 tbsp cream. Toss over a high heat until the butter melts. Leave to cool.

3 Preheat the grill. Beat the egg yolks with 1 tbsp cream and seasoning. Stir in the fish mixture. Put the egg whites into a clean, grease-free bowl and whisk until they form stiff peaks; fold into the yolks.

4 Heat the remaining butter in an omelette pan. Fry the egg mixture, but make sure it remains fairly fluid. Do not fold over. Slide it on to a flameproof serving dish.

5 Blend together the cheese and remaining fresh cream, then spread on top of the omelette and brown under the grill. Serve immediately with a rocket salad.

Serves 2

Spanish Omelette

Hands-on time: 15 minutes
Cooking time: about 45 minutes

900g (2lb) potatoes, peeled and
   left whole

3-4 tbsp vegetable oil

1 onion, finely sliced

8 medium eggs

3 tbsp freshly chopped flat-leafed parsley

3 streaky bacon rashers

salt and freshly ground black pepper

green salad to serve

1 Add the potatoes to a pan of cold
   salted water, bring to the boil, reduce
   the heat and simmer for 15-20 minutes
   or until almost cooked. Drain and
   leave until cool enough to handle,
   then slice thickly.

2 Heat 1 tbsp oil in an 18cm (7in) non-
   stick frying pan (suitable for use
   under the grill). Add the onion and fry
   gently for 7-10 minutes until softened.
   Take the pan off the heat and put to
   one side.

3 Lightly beat the eggs in a bowl and
   season well.

4 Preheat the grill. Heat the remaining
   oil in the frying pan, then layer
   the potato slices, onion and 2 tbsp
   chopped parsley in the pan. Pour in
   the beaten eggs and cook for 5-10
   minutes until the omelette is firm
   underneath. Meanwhile, grill the
   bacon until golden and crisp, and
   then break into pieces.

5 Put the omelette in the pan under
   the grill for 2-3 minutes until the
   top is just set. Scatter the bacon and
   remaining chopped parsley over the
   surface. Serve cut into wedges, with
   a green salad.

Eggs Benedict

Hands-on time: 15 minutes
Cooking time: 10 minutes

4 slices bread

4 medium eggs

150ml (¼ pint) hollandaise sauce

4 thin slices lean ham

fresh parsley sprigs to garnish

1 Toast the bread on both sides. Poach the eggs. Gently warm the hollandaise sauce.
2 Top each slice of toast with a folded slice of ham, then with a poached egg. Finally, coat the eggs with hollandaise sauce.
3 Garnish each with a sprig of parsley and serve.

SAVE EFFORT

For a delicious alternative recipe try **Eggs Florentine**:

Cook 900g (2lb) washed spinach in a pan with a little salt until tender. Drain well, chop and reheat with 15g (½oz) butter. Melt 25g (1oz) butter, stir in 3 tbsp plain flour and cook, stirring, until thickened. Add 50g (2oz) grated Gruyère or Cheddar and season. Do not allow to boil. Poach the eggs. Put the spinach into an ovenproof dish, arrange the eggs on top and pour the cheese sauce over them. Sprinkle with 25g (1oz) grated cheese and brown under the grill.

Serves 4

Perfect Scrambled Eggs

There are numerous ways to cook with eggs – from the simplest techniques such as boiling, poaching and scrambling, to more complex techniques such as making omelettes, soufflés and meringues. Follow these instructions for scrambled eggs with perfect results.

1. Allow 2 eggs per person. Break the eggs into a bowl, then beat well but lightly with a fork and season with salt and freshly ground black pepper.

2. Melt a knob of butter in a small heavy-based pan over a low heat – use a heat diffuser if necessary. (Using a non-stick pan minimises the amount of butter you need to use.)

3. Pour in the eggs and start stirring immediately, using a wooden spoon or a flat-headed spatula to break up the lumps as they form. Keep the eggs moving about as much as possible during cooking.

4 As the eggs start to set, scrape the
   bottom of the pan to keep the eggs
   from overcooking and to break up
   any larger lumps that may form.
   Your aim is to have a smooth
   mixture with no noticeable lumps.
5 Scrambled eggs may be well
   cooked and firm, or 'loose' and
   runny; this is a matter of taste.
   They will continue to cook when
   taken off the heat, so remove them
   when they are still softer than you
   want to serve them.

SAVE EFFORT

Microwave scrambled eggs
Put the eggs, milk, if you like, and
the butter into a bowl and beat well.
Microwave on full power (850W) for
1 minute (the mixture should be just
starting to set around the edges),
then beat again. Microwave again at
full power for 2-3 minutes, stirring
every 30 seconds, until the eggs are
cooked the way you like them.

Scrambled Eggs with Smoked Salmon

Hands-on time: 10 minutes
Cooking time: 5 minutes

6 large eggs

25g (1oz) butter, plus extra to spread

100g (3½oz) mascarpone

125g pack smoked salmon, sliced, or smoked salmon trimmings

6 slices sourdough or rye bread, toasted, buttered and cut into slim rectangles for soldiers

salt and freshly ground black pepper

1 Crack the eggs into a jug and lightly beat together. Season well.

2 Melt the butter in a non-stick pan over a low heat. Add the eggs and stir constantly until the mixture thickens. Add the mascarpone and season well. Cook for 1–2 minutes longer, until the mixture just becomes firm, then fold in the smoked salmon. Serve at once with toasted bread soldiers.

Serves 4

Poached Eggs with Mushrooms

TAKE 5

🍴 **Hands-on time:** 15 minutes
Cooking time: 20 minutes

8 medium-sized flat or
   portabella mushrooms

25g (1oz) butter

8 medium eggs

225g (8oz) baby spinach leaves

4 level tsp (20g) fresh pesto

1 Preheat the oven to 200°C (180°C
   fan oven) mark 6. Arrange the
   mushrooms in a single layer in a small
   roasting tin and dot with the butter.
   Roast for 15 minutes or until golden
   brown and soft.

2 Meanwhile, bring a wide shallow
   pan of water to the boil. When the
   mushrooms are half-cooked and the
   water is bubbling furiously, break the
   eggs into the pan, spaced well apart,
   then take the pan off the heat. The eggs
   will take about 6 minutes to cook.

3 When the mushrooms are tender, put
   them on a warmed plate, cover and
   rput back into the turned-off oven to
   keep warm.

4 Put the roasting tin over a medium
   heat on the hob and add the spinach.
   Cook, stirring, for about 30 seconds or
   until the spinach has just started
   to wilt.

5 The eggs should be set by now,
   so divide the mushrooms among
   four warmed plates and top with a
   little spinach, a poached egg and a
   teaspoonful of pesto.

HEALTHY TIP

Eggs once had a bad press with
many people believing (wrongly)
that they raised blood cholesterol
levels. However, scientists have
found that most people can safely
eat up to two eggs a day without any
adverse effect on their cholesterol
levels.

Baked Eggs

Hands-on time: 10 minutes
Cooking time: 15 minutes

2 tbsp olive oil

125g (4oz) mushrooms, chopped

225g (8oz) fresh spinach

2 medium eggs

2 tbsp single cream

salt and freshly ground black pepper

HEALTHY TIP

Spinach is rich in iron, which is better absorbed when you consume a vitamin C-rich source (such as orange juice) at the same meal.

1 Preheat the oven to 200°C (180°C fan oven) mark 6. Heat the oil in a large frying pan. Add the mushrooms and stir-fry for 30 seconds. Add the spinach and stir-fry until wilted. Season to taste, then divide the mixture between two shallow ovenproof dishes.

2 Carefully break an egg into the centre of each dish, then spoon 1 tbsp single cream over it.

3 Cook in the oven for about 12 minutes or until just set – the eggs will continue to cook a little once they're out of the oven. Grind a little more black pepper over the top, if you like, and serve.

Serves 2

Mixed Mushroom Frittata

🍴 **Hands-on time:** 15 minutes
Cooking time: about 20 minutes

1 tbsp olive oil

300g (11oz) mixed mushrooms, sliced

2 tbsp freshly chopped thyme

grated zest and juice of ½ lemon

50g (2oz) watercress, chopped

6 medium eggs, beaten

salt and freshly ground black pepper

crisp green salad and wholegrain bread
to serve

HEALTHY TIP

Eggs are a good source of protein
– 2 eggs supply roughly one-third
of an adult's daily requirement – as
well as vitamins A and D.

1 Heat the oil in a large deep frying pan (suitable for use under the grill) over a medium heat. Add the mushrooms and thyme and stir-fry for 4–5 minutes until starting to soften and brown. Stir in the lemon zest and juice, then bubble or 1 minute. Reduce the heat.

2 Preheat the grill. Add the watercress to the beaten eggs, season with salt and ground black pepper and pour into the pan. Cook on the hob for 7–8 minutes until the sides and base are firm but the centre is still a little soft.

3 Transfer to the grill and cook for 4–5 minutes until just set. Cut the frittata into wedges and serve with a crisp green salad and chunks of wholegrain bread.

Serves 4

Perfect Eggs

Follow these tried and tested steps for poached, coddled and boiled eggs.

Poaching

1 Heat about 8cm (3¼in) of lightly salted water in a shallow frying pan to a bare simmer. Crack a very fresh egg into a cup, then slip it into the water. (The whites in a fresh egg are firmer and will form a 'nest' for the yolk while older egg whites are watery and spread out in the pan.)

2 Cook for 3–4 minutes until the white is barely set. Remove the egg with a slotted spoon and drain on kitchen paper.

Perfect coddling

1 Using a slotted spoon, gently lower the whole eggs into a pan of simmering water, then take the pan off the heat.

2 Leave the eggs to stand in the water for 4–5 minutes, where they will cook gently with the residual heat of the water.

2

Perfect boiled eggs

There are two ways to boil an egg: starting in boiling water or starting in cold water. Both work well as long as you follow certain rules:

❑ The egg must be at room temperature

❑ For both methods, cover the eggs with water, plus 2.5cm (1in) or so extra

❑ If starting in boiling water, use an 'egg pick', if you like, to pierce the broad end of the shell. This allows air in the pocket at the base of the egg to escape and avoids cracking

❑ Gently lower in the eggs using a long spoon to avoid cracking them

❑ Cook at a simmer rather than a rolling boil

Boiling: method 1

1 Bring a small pan of water to the boil. Once the water is boiling, add a medium egg. For a soft-boiled egg, cook for 6 minutes; for a salad egg, cook for 8 minutes; and for a hard-boiled egg, cook for 10 minutes.

2 Remove the egg from the water with a slotted spoon and serve.

Boiling: method 2

1 Put a medium egg in a small pan and cover with cold water. Put on a lid and bring to the boil. When the water begins to boil, remove the lid and cook for 2 minutes for a soft-boiled egg, 5 minutes for a salad egg, and 7 minutes for a

Duck Egg and Asparagus Dippers

Hands-on time: 15 minutes
Cooking time: about 6 minutes

600g (1lb 5oz) asparagus spears
(not the fine variety)
6 duck eggs
extra virgin olive oil, to drizzle
salt and freshly ground black pepper
sourdough bread (optional) to serve

1 Holding both ends of an asparagus spear in your hands, bend gently until it snaps. Discard the woody end (or keep to make soups or stocks). Trim all the remaining spears to this length. Use a vegetable peeler to shave any knobbly or woody bits below the tip of each spear.

2 Divide the asparagus equally into six piles, then tie each neatly into a bundle with string.

3 Bring two medium pans of water to the boil. Add the eggs to one pan and simmer for exactly 5½ minutes. Add the asparagus bundles to the other pan and cook for 1 minute until just tender. Drain the asparagus and leave to steam-dry in the colander for 3 minutes. Drain the eggs.

4 Put one asparagus bundle on each plate, drizzle with a little extra virgin olive oil and season with salt and ground black pepper. Serve with the eggs, plus a slice of sourdough bread, if you like.

SAVE TIME

Prepare the asparagus to the end of step 2 up to 2 hours in advance. Chill the bundles, then complete the recipe to serve.

Serves 6

Huevos Rancheros

Hands-on time: 10 minutes
Cooking time: about 15 minutes

1 tbsp vegetable oil

1 medium red onion, finely sliced

1 each yellow and red pepper, deseeded and finely sliced

1 red chilli, deseeded and finely sliced

2 × 400g tins chopped tomatoes

½ tsp dried mixed herbs

4 large eggs

small handful flat leafed parsley, roughly chopped

crusty bread, to serve

1 Heat the oil in a large frying pan over a high heat. Fry the onion, peppers and chilli for 3 minutes until just softened. Add the tomatoes and dried herbs. Season and simmer for 3 minutes.

2 Break an egg into a small cup. Use a wooden spoon to scrape a hole in the tomato mixture, then quickly drop in the egg. Repeat with the remaining eggs, spacing evenly around the tomato mixture. Cover and simmer for 3-5 minutes until the eggs are just set. Sprinkle with parsley and serve with crusty bread.

Serves 6

Sweet Plates

Perfect Batters

Batters can serve a number of purposes, and are remarkably versatile for something so simple. All you need to remember when working with them is to mix quickly and lightly.

Pancakes

To make eight pancakes, you will need:
125g (4oz) plain flour, a pinch of salt, 1 medium egg, 300ml (½ pint) milk, oil and butter to fry.

1 Sift the flour and salt into a bowl, make a well in the centre and whisk in the egg. Gradually beat in the milk to make a smooth batter, then leave to stand for 20 minutes.
2 Heat a heavy-based frying pan and coat lightly with fat. Pour in a little batter and tilt the pan to coat the bottom thinly and evenly.
3 Cook over a moderately high heat for 1 minute or until golden. Turn over carefully and cook the other side for 30 seconds–1 minute.

Drop Scones

For 15–18 pancakes, you will need:
125g (4oz) self-raising flour,
2 tbsp caster sugar, 1 medium egg,
beaten, 150ml (¼ pint) milk and a
little vegetable oil to grease.

1. Mix the flour and sugar in a bowl.
   Make a well in the centre and
   mix in the egg and a little milk to
   achieve the consistency of thick
   cream.
2. Oil a griddle or heavy frying pan
   and heat it until medium-hot. Drop
   some of the batter in small rounds
   on to the griddle or pan and cook
   at a steady heat until bubbles rise
   to the surface – 2–3 minutes.
3. Turn and cook for 2–3 minutes
   more, then remove to a clean
   teatowel. Cover with another clean
   teatowel to keep them moist, and
   continue cooking the scones until
   you have used all the batter.

2

3

Lemon and Blueberry Pancakes

Hands-on time: 15 minutes
Cooking time: about 15 minutes

125g (4oz) wholemeal plain flour

1 tsp baking powder

¼ tsp bicarbonate of soda

2 tbsp golden caster sugar

finely grated zest of 1 lemon

125g (4oz) natural yogurt

2 tbsp milk

2 medium eggs

40g (1½oz) butter

100g (3½oz) blueberries

1 tsp sunflower oil

natural yogurt and fruit compôte
   to serve

1 Sift the flour, baking powder and bicarbonate of soda into a bowl. Add the sugar and lemon zest. Pour in the yogurt and milk. Break the eggs into the mixture and whisk together.

2 Melt 25g (1oz) butter in a pan, add to the bowl with the blueberries and stir everything together.

3 Heat a dot of butter with the oil in a frying pan over a medium heat until hot. Add four large spoonfuls of the mixture to the pan to make four pancakes. After about 2 minutes, flip them over and cook for 1–2 minutes. Repeat with the remaining mixture, adding a dot more butter each time.

4 Serve with natural yogurt and some fruit compôte.

SAVE EFFORT

Instead of fresh blueberries and lemon, use 100g (3½oz) chopped ready-to-eat dried apricots and 2 tsp grated fresh root ginger.

American-style Pancakes

Hands-on time: 10 minutes, plus standing
Cooking time: about 15 minutes

175g (6oz) self-raising flour
1 tsp baking powder
1 tsp bicarbonate of soda
a pinch of salt
50g (2oz) caster sugar
1 large egg, beaten
300ml (½ pint) buttermilk
50g (2oz) butter, melted and
    cooled slightly, plus extra for frying
milk (optional)
crispy streaky bacon and maple syrup
    to serve

1 In a bowl, sift together the flour,
baking powder and bicarbonate
of soda with a pinch of salt. Stir in
the sugar.

2 Combine the egg, buttermilk and
butter, and gradually whisk into the
flour to make a smooth batter – it
should be the consistency of thick
double cream, so add a drop of
milk if necessary. Leave to stand
for 5 minutes.

3 Put a large frying pan over a medium
heat until hot. Brush the surface with
a little melted butter. Pour about 2
tbsp of the mixture into the pan to
form a 10cm (4in) circle – the mixture
should spread naturally to that size if
it is the right consistency. Cook for 2
minutes or until small holes appear
on the surface, then turn over and
cook for 1–2 minutes more or until
golden and cooked through. Do this in
batches, depending on the size of your
pan and regreasing the bottom when
necessary. Serve warm with plenty of
crispy streaky bacon and maple syrup.

Makes 12

Cinnamon Pancakes

Hands-on time: 5 minutes, plus standing
Cooking time: 20 minutes

150g (5oz) plain flour

½ tsp ground cinnamon

1 medium egg

300ml (½ pint) skimmed milk

olive oil to fry

fruit compote or sugar and Greek yogurt
   to serve

SAVE MONEY

If you don't have any fruit compote
or yogurt, try serving the pancakes
with sliced bananas and vanilla ice
cream instead.

1 Whisk the flour, cinnamon, egg and milk together in a large bowl to make a smooth batter. Leave to stand for 20 minutes.

2 Heat a heavy-based frying pan over a medium heat. When the pan is really hot, add 1 tsp oil, pour in a ladleful of batter and tilt the pan to coat the bottom with an even layer. Cook for 1 minute or until golden. Flip over and cook for 1 minute. Repeat with the remaining batter, adding more oil if necessary, to make six pancakes. Serve with a fruit compote or a sprinkling of sugar, and a dollop of yogurt.

Serves 6

Scotch Pancakes

Hands-on time: 10 minutes
Cooking time: about 18 minutes

125g (4oz) self-raising flour

2 tbsp caster sugar

1 medium egg, beaten

150ml (¼ pint) milk

vegetable oil to grease

butter, or whipped cream and jam,
  to serve

1 Mix the flour and sugar together in a bowl. Make a well in the centre and mix in the egg, with enough of the milk to make a batter the consistency of thick cream – working as quickly and lightly as possible.

2 Cook the mixture in batches: drop spoonfuls on to an oiled hot griddle or heavy-based frying pan. Keep the griddle at a steady heat and when bubbles rise to the surface of the scone and burst, after 2–3 minutes, turn over with a palette knife.

3 Cook for 2–3 minutes more until golden brown on the other side.

4 Put the cooked drop scones on a clean teatowel and cover with another teatowel to keep them moist. Serve warm, with butter, or whipped cream and jam.

Makes 15–18

Crêpes Suzette

Hands-on time: 20 minutes, plus standing
Cooking time: 15 minutes

1 quantity crêpe batter (see page 92)

1 tsp golden icing sugar

grated zest of ½ orange

a knob of butter, plus extra to fry

2 tbsp brandy

For the orange sauce

50g (2oz) golden caster sugar

50g (2oz) butter

juice of 2 oranges

grated zest of 1 lemon

3 tbsp Cointreau

1 Flavour the crêpe batter with the icing sugar and orange zest, then leave to stand for 30 minutes. Just before cooking the crêpes, melt the knob of butter and stir it into the batter.

2 To cook the crêpes, heat a small amount of butter in a 15–18cm (6–7in) heavy-based frying pan. Pour in just enough batter to cover the bottom, swirling it to coat. Cook over a medium heat for about 1 minute or until the crêpe is golden underneath. Using a palette knife, flip it over and cook briefly on the other side. Lift on to a plate, cover with greaseproof paper and keep warm while you cook the others in the same way, interleaving each with a square of greaseproof paper to keep them separated.

3 To make the orange sauce, put the sugar into a large heavy-based frying pan and heat gently, shaking the pan occasionally, until the sugar has dissolved and turned golden brown. Remove from the heat and add the butter, orange juice and lemon zest. Put the pan back on to the heat, and stir the sauce until it begins to simmer. Add the Cointreau.

4 Fold each crêpe in half and then in half again. Put all the crêpes back into the pan and simmer for a few minutes to reheat, spooning the sauce over them.

5 To flambé, warm the brandy and pour it over the crêpes. Using a taper and standing well clear, ignite the brandy. When the flame dies down, serve immediately.

Serves 4

Waffles

Hands-on time: 5 minutes
Cooking time: 16 minutes

125g (4oz) self-raising flour

a pinch of salt

1 tbsp caster sugar

1 medium egg, separated

25g (1oz) butter, melted

150ml (¼ pint) milk

½ tsp vanilla flavouring (optional)

butter and golden or maple syrup
to serve

1 Heat the waffle iron according to the manufacturer's instructions.

2 Mix the flour, salt and sugar together in a bowl. Add the egg yolk, melted butter, milk and flavouring, if you like, and beat to give a smooth coating batter.

3 Put the egg white into a clean, grease-free bowl and whisk until it forms stiff peaks; fold into the batter. Pour just enough batter into the iron to run over the surface.

4 Close the iron and cook for 2–3 minutes, turning the iron if using a non-electric type. When the waffle is cooked, it should be golden brown and crisp and easily removed from the iron – if it sticks, cook for a minute longer. Cook the remainder in the same way.

5 Serve immediately with butter and golden or maple syrup. Alternatively, layer the waffles with whipped cream or vanilla ice cream and fresh fruit.

French Toast

Hands-on time: 5 minutes
Cooking time: 10 minutes

2 medium eggs

150ml (¼ pint) semi-skimmed milk

a generous pinch of freshly grated nutmeg or ground cinnamon

4 slices white bread, or fruit bread, crusts removed and each slice cut into four fingers

50g (2oz) butter

vegetable oil for frying

1 tbsp golden caster sugar

1 Put the eggs, milk and nutmeg or cinnamon into a shallow dish and beat together.

2 Dip the pieces of bread into the mixture, coating them well.

3 Heat half the butter with 1 tbsp oil in a heavy-based frying pan. When the butter is foaming, fry the egg-coated bread pieces in batches, until golden on both sides, adding more butter and oil as needed. Sprinkle with sugar and serve.

SAVE MONEY

Use leftover bread for this tasty breakfast or brunch dish. For a savoury version, use white bread and omit the spice and sugar; serve with tomato ketchup, or with bacon and maple syrup.

Serves 4

Orange Eggy Bread

Hands-on time: 10 minutes
Cooking time: 15 minutes

2 large eggs

150ml (¼ pint) milk

finely grated zest of 1 orange

50g (2oz) butter

8 slices raisin bread, halved diagonally

1 tbsp caster sugar

vanilla ice cream and orange segments
to serve (optional)

1 Lightly whisk the eggs, milk and orange zest together in a bowl.
2 Heat the butter in a large frying pan over a medium heat. Dip the slices of raisin bread into the egg mixture, then fry on both sides until golden.
3 Sprinkle the bread with the sugar and serve immediately with ice cream and orange slices, if you like.

Sandwiches and Savouries

Oatmeal Soda Bread

Hands-on time: 15 minutes
Cooking time: 25 minutes, plus cooling

25g (1oz) butter, plus extra to grease

275g (10oz) plain wholemeal flour

175g (6oz) coarse oatmeal

2 tsp cream of tartar

1 tsp salt

about 300ml (10fl oz) milk and
  water, mixed

butter to serve

1 Preheat the oven to 220°C (200°C fan oven) mark 7. Grease a 900g (2lb) loaf tin and base-line with baking parchment.

2 Mix together all the dry ingredients in a bowl. Rub in the butter.

3 Add the milk and water to bind to a soft dough. Spoon into the prepared loaf tin.

4 Bake for 25 minutes or until golden brown and well risen. Turn out and leave to cool slightly on a wire rack. Serve with butter. It is best eaten on the day of making.

HEALTHY TIP

This bread contains oatmeal, which is rich in betaglucan, a soluble fibre that helps lower levels of cholesterol in the bloodstream. It also helps make you feel full longer and control blood sugar levels. Oats are also a good source of B vitamins and vitamin E.

Makes 1 loaf – cuts into about 10 slices

White Farmhouse Loaf

Hands-on time: 10 minutes, plus kneading
Cooking time: as per your machine, plus cooling

500g (1lb 2oz) strong white bread flour,
   plus extra to sprinkle

1 tbsp caster sugar

2 tbsp milk powder

1½ tsp salt

25g (1oz) butter

1 tsp easy-blend dried yeast

1 Put the ingredients, including 350ml (12fl oz) water, into the bread-maker's bucket, following the order and method specified in the manual.

2 Fit the bucket into the bread-maker and set to the basic program with a crust of your choice. Press 'Start'.

3 Just before baking begins, brush the top of the dough with water and sprinkle with flour. If preferred, slash the top of the bread lengthways with a sharp knife, taking care not to scratch the bucket.

4 After baking, remove the bucket from the machine, then turn out the loaf on to a wire rack to cool.

Makes 1 loaf – cuts into about 12 slices

Dos and don'ts of breadmaking

1 Make sure shaped dough has risen sufficiently – usually to double.

2 Always oil or flour the loaf tin, or baking sheet, to prevent sticking.

3 Make sure the oven is at the correct temperature before you begin baking.

4 Bake on a preheated ceramic baking stone (from good kitchen shops) if possible, even if the bread is in a loaf tin. The heat of the stone will give the bread a crisp base.

5 If baked bread is left for too long either in the loaf tin or on the baking sheet, steam will gather and, as a result, the underneath will start to become soggy. To prevent this, always remove the loaf immediately and put it on a wire rack. Then leave it to cool completely before slicing, as you like.

Dos and don'ts of machine-baked bread

1. Use recipes that have been designed for bread machine use only, as conventional bread recipes use different quantities of ingredients and are not converted easily.

2. Measure out all the ingredients carefully, as exact quantities are essential for a perfect loaf.

3. Always follow the bread machine instructions carefully; it is essential that the ingredients go into the machine in the order stated, as the yeast must not come into contact with the liquid until the machine begins to mix.

4. Avoid lifting the lid during the rising and baking cycles, as this may cause the loaf to sink.

5. The loaf is best removed from the machine as soon as it is baked, otherwise it will become soggy.

Herby Mushrooms on Toast

Hands-on time: 20 minutes
Cooking time: about 20 minutes.

4 large eggs

25g (1oz) butter

4 shallots, finely diced

3 garlic cloves, crushed

600g (1lb 5oz) chestnut mushrooms, chopped

2 tbsp marsala or sherry, optional

2 tbsp each chopped fresh tarragon and parsley

4 sourdough bread slices, freshly toasted

green salad, to serve

1 Start by bringing a medium pan of water to the boil. Crack an egg into a cup or ramekin. Swirl the boiling water, then tip in the egg. Quickly crack another egg and add to the water. Simmer for 3-4 minutes until the egg whites are set and the yolk remains soft (to check, lift the egg out and gently prod with your finger). Transfer the cooked eggs to a shallow dish of warm water. Repeat with remaining eggs.

2 Melt the butter in a large frying pan and cook the shallots and garlic for 10 minutes. Turn up the heat, add the mushrooms and fry for 5 minutes. Add the marsala or sherry, if using, then stir in the herbs. Check the seasoning.

3 Top each piece of toast with a pile of mushrooms. Lift the eggs out of water and dab dry with kitchen paper. Put an egg on each toast and serve with a green salad.

Serves 4

Mozzarella Mushrooms

Hands-on time: about 3 minutes
Cooking time: about 20 minutes

8 large portabella mushrooms
8 slices marinated red pepper
8 fresh basil leaves
150g (5oz) mozzarella cheese,
    cut into 8 slices
4 English muffins, halved
salt and freshly ground black pepper
green salad to serve

HEALTHY TIP

Mushrooms are an excellent source of potassium – a mineral that helps lower elevated blood pressure and reduces the risk of stroke. One medium portabella mushroom has even more potassium than a banana or a glass of orange juice. Mushrooms contain antioxidant nutrients that help inhibit the development of cancers of the breast and prostate.

1 Preheat the oven to 200°C (180°C fan oven) mark 6. Lay the mushrooms side by side in a roasting tin and season with salt and ground black pepper. Top each mushroom with a slice of red pepper and a basil leaf. Lay a slice of mozzarella on top of each mushroom and season again.

2 Roast for 15–20 minutes or until the mushrooms are tender and the cheese has melted.

3 Meanwhile, toast the muffin halves until golden. Put a mozzarella mushroom on top of each muffin half. Serve immediately with a green salad.

Serves 4

Low-GI Beans on Toast

Hands-on time: 5 minutes
Cooking time: 10 minutes

1 tbsp olive oil

2 garlic cloves, finely sliced

400g can borlotti or cannellini beans, drained and rinsed

400g can chickpeas, drained and rinsed

400g can chopped tomatoes

2 fresh rosemary sprigs

4 slices sourdough or Granary bread

25g (1oz) Parmesan

1 Heat the oil in a pan over a low heat, add the garlic and cook for 1 minute, stirring gently.

2 Add the beans and chickpeas to the pan with the tomatoes, and bring to the boil. Strip the leaves from the rosemary sprigs, then chop finely and add to the pan. Reduce the heat and simmer for 8-10 minutes until thickened.

3 Meanwhile, toast the bread and put on to plates. Grate the Parmesan into the bean mixture, stir once, then spoon over the toast and serve immediately.

Serves 4

Traditional Kippers

🍴 **Hands-on time:** about 5 minutes
Cooking time: about 15 minutes

2 kippers

butter, freshly chopped parsley and toast to serve

1 Cook the kippers by one of the following methods:
Grill the kippers for 5 minutes or put into a jug of boiling water and leave in a warm place for 5-10 minutes; alternatively, wrap them in foil and cook them in an oven preheated to 190°C (170°C fan oven) mark 5 for 10-15 minutes.

2 Serve with butter, parsley and toast.

SAVE EFFORT

Kippers are whole herrings that have been split and opened out flat. They are lightly brined, then cold-smoked, which already gives them a rich flavour.

Serves 2

Smoked Haddock Kedgeree

Hands-on time: 30 minutes, plus chilling (optional)
Cooking time: about 15 minutes

175g (6oz) long-grain rice
450g (1lb) smoked haddock fillets
2 medium eggs, hard-boiled
   and shelled
75g (3oz) butter
salt and cayenne pepper
freshly chopped parsley to garnish

1 Cook the rice in a pan of fast-boiling salted water until tender. Drain well and rinse under cold water.

2 Meanwhile, put the haddock in a large frying pan with just enough water to cover. Bring to simmering point, then simmer for 10–15 minutes until tender. Drain, skin and flake the fish, discarding the bones.

3 Chop one egg and slice the other into rings. Melt the butter in a pan, add the cooked rice, fish, chopped egg, salt and cayenne pepper, and stir over a medium heat for 5 minutes or until hot. Pile on to a warmed serving dish and garnish with parsley and the sliced egg.

Serves 4

Welsh Rarebit

Hands-on time: 15 minutes
Cooking time: about 15 minutes

400g can chopped tomatoes

½ tbsp tomato purée

1 small shallot, finely sliced

175g (6oz) Caerphilly or mature
   Cheddar, grated

½ tsp English mustard

50ml (2fl oz) ale

few dashes Worcestershire sauce

1 large egg yolk

1½ tbsp finely chopped fresh parsley

8 crumpets

salt and freshly ground black pepper

crisp green salad to serve

1 Put the canned tomatoes, tomato
   purée and shallot into a small pan.
   Bring to the boil, then reduce the heat
   and simmer for 10 minutes. Check the
   seasoning.

2 Meanwhile, mix the cheese, mustard,
   ale, Worcestershire sauce, egg yolk,
   parsley and some seasoning together
   in a bowl.

3 Preheat the grill to medium. Arrange
   the crumpets on a baking sheet and
   toast until golden. Divide and spread
   the tomato sauce equally over the
   toasted crumpets, then top each
   with an equal amount of the cheese
   mixture. Grill for 3–5 minutes until
   bubbling and golden. Serve with a
   crisp green salad.

Serves 4

BLT-topped Bagels with Hollandaise Sauce

Hands-on time: 15 minutes
Cooking time: 8 minutes

3 large bagels, cut in half horizontally

25g (1oz) butter, softened

12 smoked streaky bacon rashers,
   rind removed

2 tsp olive oil

3 tomatoes, cut into thick slices

150ml (¼ pint) bought hollandaise sauce

75g (3oz) rocket

freshly ground black pepper

1 Preheat the grill to high, then grill the halved bagels until golden. Spread generously with the butter. Cover the bagels with a piece of foil and keep them warm. Grill the bacon for 2–3 minutes until crisp, then keep warm.

2 Heat the oil in a small frying pan until very hot and fry the tomatoes for about 1 minute until lightly charred. Put the hollandaise sauce in a small pan and heat gently.

3 To assemble, top the warm bagels with a few rocket leaves, the tomatoes and bacon. Spoon the warm hollandaise sauce over the bacon and season with pepper. Serve immediately.

Serves 6

Croque Monsieur

TAKE 5

🍴 **Hands-on time:** 5 minutes
Cooking time: 8 minutes

4 slices white bread

butter, softened, to spread, plus extra for frying

Dijon mustard, to taste

125g (4oz) Gruyère

4 slices ham

1 Spread each slice of bread on both sides with the butter. Then spread one side of two slices of bread with a little Dijon mustard.

2 Divide the cheese and ham between the two mustard-spread bread slices. Top each with the remaining bread and press down.

3 Heat a griddle with a little butter until hot and fry the sandwiches for 2–3 minutes on each side until golden and crispy and the cheese starts to melt. Slice in half and serve immediately.

Smoothies and Drinks

Perfect Smoothies and Purées

Fruit, whether cooked or raw, can be transformed into a smooth sauce by puréeing. It also makes a healthy breakfast or snack that is bursting with flavour when used in a smoothie.

Making smoothies

To serve four, you will need:
4 passion fruit, 150ml (¼ pint) low-fat yogurt, 4 bananas, 225g (8oz) grapes.

1 Halve the passion fruit and scoop the pulp into a blender. Add the remaining ingredients. Crush 8 ice cubes and add to the blender.
2 Process until smooth and pour into glasses. Serve immediately.

Puréeing in a blender

Some fruit can be puréed raw, while others are better cooked. Wait until cooked fruit cools.

1. Blend a spoonful of fruit until smooth, then add another spoonful and blend. Add rest of fruit in batches.
2. For a very smooth purée, pass through a fine sieve.

Banana Vitality Shake

Preparation time: 10 minutes

25g (1oz) whole shelled almonds

1 large ripe banana

150ml (¼ pint) low-fat milk

150ml (¼ pint) low-fat natural yogurt

8g sachet powdered egg white

2 tsp wheatgerm

1–2 tsp maple syrup

a pinch of freshly grated nutmeg

1 Grind the almonds in a spice grinder or food processor – the mixture needs to be very fine to get a good blend.

2 Peel and roughly chop the banana, then put into a blender with the ground almonds. Add the milk, yogurt, powdered egg white and wheatgerm to the blender and whiz for a few seconds until smooth.

3 Add maple syrup to taste, then pour into two glasses and serve immediately, sprinkled with nutmeg.

HEALTHY TIP

A good source of protein, calcium, carbohydrates and B vitamins, this shake makes a highly nutritious supplement for regular exercisers. Almonds add healthy monounsaturated fats as well as vitamin E and iron.

Serves 2, makes 600ml (1 pint)

Creamy Dairy-free Banana

TAKE 5

🍴 Hands-on time: 5 minutes

1 large ripe banana

125g (4oz) silken tofu, well chilled

175ml (6fl oz) unsweetened soya milk, well chilled

2 tsp thick honey

a few drops of vanilla extract

1. Peel the banana and slice thickly. Put into a blender.

2. Drain the tofu, mash lightly with a fork and add to the blender.

3. Pour in the milk and add the honey with a few drops of vanilla extract. Whiz for a few seconds until thick and smooth. Pour the smoothie into a large glass and serve.

SAVE EFFORT

Silken tofu is very smooth and is the best for blending in drinks. It is available fresh or vacuum-packed in cartons. Firmer types can be used but give a grainier texture when blended.

Serves 1, makes 400ml (14fl oz)

Breakfast Smoothie

TAKE
5

Hands-on time: 5 minutes

200ml (7fl oz) semi-skimmed milk

200g (7oz) natural yogurt

125g (4oz) mix of frozen berries – we
used a mix of blackberries, blueberries
and blackcurrants

15g (½oz) rolled oats

2 tbsp runny honey

1 Put all the ingredients into a blender
and whiz until smooth. Pour into two
tall glasses and serve.

SAVE TIME

If you prefer to have your breakfast
ready to go, make a double
smoothie batch in the evening, then
transfer the mixture to a jug, cover
and chill for up to two days. Simply
stir before serving.

Serves 2

Perfect Smoothie Boosts

There are many ingredients that you can add to smoothies
if you have specific nutritional requirements.

Acidophilus

A probiotic: 'friendly' bacteria that
promote good health. Acidophilus
is most beneficial when taken if you
are suffering from diarrhoea or after
a course of antibiotics, or if you have
digestive problems such as irritable
bowel syndrome (IBS). Available
from most chemists and health
shops in capsule form, which usually
need to be kept in the refrigerator.
Probiotics are now included in some
ready-made drinks and yogurt
products.

Bee Pollen

See page 148 for details and advice
on where you can buy bee pollen.

Brewers' yeast

A by-product of beer brewing,
brewers' yeast is exceptionally rich in
B vitamins, with high levels of iron,
zinc, magnesium and potassium.
Highly concentrated and an excellent
pick-me-up, but the flavour is strong
and needs to be mixed with other
ingredients. Available as pills or
powder.
Warning: it is high in purines so
should be avoided by gout sufferers.

Echinacea

Recommended by herbalists for
many years, echinacea is a native
plant of North America, taken to
support a healthy immune system.
A great all-rounder with anti-viral
and anti-bacterial properties. Comes
in capsules and in extracts taken in
drops, so is easy to add to smoothies.

Warning: not recommended for use during pregnancy or when breastfeeding.

Eggs

High in protein, but eggs also contain cholesterol so you might need to limit your intake; ask your GP. Egg white powder is low in fat and can be added to smoothies for a protein boost. Always use the freshest eggs for smoothies.

Warning: raw egg should not be eaten by the elderly, children, babies, pregnant women or those with an impaired immune system as there can be a risk of contracting salmonella.

Ginseng

Derived from the roots of a plant grown in Russia, Korea and China. The active constituents are ginsenosides, reputed to stimulate the hormones and increase energy. Available in dry root form for grinding or ready powdered.

Warning: should not be taken by those suffering from hypertension.

Nuts

Packed with nutrients, nuts are a concentrated form of protein and are rich in antioxidants, vitamins B1, B6 and E, and many minerals. Brazil nuts are one of the best sources of selenium in the diet. Nuts do have a high fat content, but this is mostly unsaturated fat. Walnuts are particularly high in omega-3, an essential fatty acid that is needed for healthy heart and brain function. Brazil, cashew, coconut, peanut and macadamia nuts contain more saturated fat, so should be used sparingly. Almonds are particularly easy to digest. Finely chop or grind the nuts just before using for maximum freshness.

Seeds

Highly nutritious, seeds contain a good supply of essential fatty acids (EFAs). Flaxseed (linseed) is particularly beneficial as it is one of the richest sources of omega-3 EFAs, with 57% more than oily fish. Pumpkin, sesame and sunflower seeds also work well in smoothies. They are best bought in small amounts as their fat content makes them go rancid quickly, so store in airtight containers in the refrigerator. Grind them just before use for maximum benefit, or use the oils – these have to be stored in the refrigerator.

Sprouting seeds

These are simply seeds from a variety of plants – such as sunflower, chickpea and mung bean – which have been given a little water and warmth and have started to grow. Sprouts are full of vitamins, minerals, proteins and carbohydrates. They are pretty soft so they whiz up easily in the blender for savoury smoothies.

Oats

Sold in the form of whole grain, rolled, flaked or ground (oatmeal), oats are high in protein, vitamin B complex, vitamin E, potassium, calcium, phosphorus, iron and zinc; they are easy to digest and can soothe the digestive tract. They are also a rich source of soluble fibre, which helps to lower high blood cholesterol levels, which in turn will help reduce the risk of heart disease. Toasted oatmeal has a nutty flavour and is ideal for smoothies.

Warning: oats should be avoided by those on a gluten-free diet.

Wheat bran and germ

Wheat bran is the outside of the wheat grain removed during milling; it is very high in fibre and adds bulk to the diet. It is bland in taste but adds a crunchy texture. Wheat germ, from the centre of the grain, is very nutritious and easy to digest, with a mild flavour. Highly perishable, store in the refrigerator once the pack is opened.

Warning: keep your intake of bran to moderate levels; large amounts can prevent vitamins and minerals from being absorbed.

Non-dairy alternatives

Soya milk and yogurt

If you are allergic to dairy products or lactose-intolerant, drinking milk may cause a variety of symptoms, including skin rashes and eczema, asthma and irritable bowel syndrome. Soya milk and yogurt are useful alternatives – look for calcium-enriched products. Good non-dairy sources of calcium suitable for adding to smoothies include dark green leafy vegetables, such as watercress and spinach, and apricots.

Silken tofu

This protein-rich dairy-free product adds a creamy texture to fruit and vegetable smoothies.

Busy Bee's Comforter

🍴 **Hands-on time:** 5 minutes

2 lemons

150ml (¼ pint) full-fat natural or soya yogurt, at room temperature

1–2 tsp thick honey

2–3 tsp bee pollen grains or equivalent in capsule form

1 Using a sharp knife, cut off the peel from one lemon, removing as much of the white pith as possible. Chop the flesh roughly, discarding any pips, and put into a blender. Squeeze the juice from the remaining lemon and add to the blender.

2 Spoon in the yogurt and whiz until smooth. Taste and sweeten with honey as necessary. Stir in the bee pollen, then pour into a glass and serve immediately.

HEALTHY TIP

You can buy bee pollen grains at specialist health-food shops and online. This drink is a very good source of protein and calcium. It contains honey, which is a source of slow-releasing sugars, and a powerful antibacterial and anti-viral ingredient. Note, this drink is unsuitable for those with an allergy to pollen, such as hayfever sufferers.

Serves 1, makes 200ml (7fl oz)

Apricot and Orange Smoothie

Hands-on time: 5 minutes, plus chilling

400g (14oz) canned apricots in natural juice

150g (5oz) apricot yogurt

200–250ml (7–9fl oz) unsweetened orange juice

1 Put the apricots, yogurt and orange juice into a blender or food processor and whiz for 1 minute or until smooth.

2 Chill well, then pour into two glasses and serve.

Serves 2, makes about 450ml (15fl oz)

Raspberry Rascal Booster

Hands-on time: 5 minutes

225g (8oz) raspberries, thawed if frozen, juices put to one side

1 medium orange

2 tsp thick honey

1 If using fresh raspberries, remove the hulls, then wash and pat the fruit dry with kitchen paper. Put two raspberries to one side for the decoration and put the rest into a blender. If the fruit has been frozen, add the juices as well.

2 Peel the orange, removing as much of the white pith as possible. Chop the flesh roughly, discarding any pips, and put into the blender. Add the honey. Whiz until smooth, then pour into a glass, decorate with the raspberries and serve immediately.

HEALTHY TIP

This refreshing drink is bursting with vitamin C and anthocyanins, which help strengthen blood vessels and boost your immune system.

Serves 1, makes 300ml (1/2 pint)

Cranberry and Mango Smoothie

🍴 **Hands-on time:** 5 minutes

1 ripe mango, stoned (see page 156)
250ml (9fl oz) cranberry juice
150g (5oz) natural yogurt

1 Peel and roughly chop the mango and put into a blender with the cranberry juice. Blend for 1 minute.
2 Add the yogurt and blend until smooth, then serve.

HEALTHY TIP

If you're on a dairy-free diet or are looking for an alternative to milk-based products, swap the yogurt for soya yogurt. Soya is a good source of essential omega-3 and omega-6 fatty acids, and can help to lower cholesterol.

Serves 2

Mangoes

1 Cut a slice to one side of the stone in the centre. Repeat on the other side.
2 Cut parallel lines into the flesh of one slice, almost to the skin. Cut another set of lines to cut the flesh into squares.
3 Press on the skin side to turn the fruit inside out, so that the flesh is thrust outwards. Cut off the chunks as close as possible to the skin. Repeat with the other half.

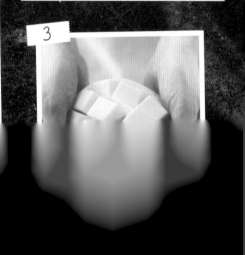

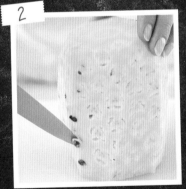

Pineapples

1. Cut off the base and crown of the pineapple, and stand the fruit on a chopping board.
2. Using a medium-sized knife, peel away a section of skin, going just deep enough to remove all or most of the hard, inedible 'eyes' on the skin. Repeat all the way around.
3. Use a small knife to cut out any remaining traces of the eyes.
4. Cut the peeled pineapple into slices.

Mango and Oat Smoothie

Hands-on time: 5 minutes

150g (5oz) natural yogurt

1 small mango, peeled, stoned
and chopped (see page 156)

2 tbsp oats

4 ice cubes

1 Put the yogurt into a blender. Put a little chopped mango to one side for the decoration, if you like, and add the remaining mango, oats and ice cubes to the yogurt. Whiz the ingredients until smooth. Serve immediately, decorated with the chopped mango.

SAVE EFFORT

If you can't find a mango, use 2 nectarines or peaches, or 175g (6oz) soft seasonal fruits such as raspberries, strawberries or blueberries instead.

Serves 2

Summer Berry Smoothie

Hands-on time: 10 minutes

2 large ripe bananas, about 450g (1lb)

150g (5oz) natural yogurt

500g (1lb 2oz) fresh or frozen
   summer berries

1 Peel and chop the bananas, then put into a blender. Add the yogurt and 150ml (¼ pint) water, then whiz until smooth. Add the berries and whiz to a purée.

2 Strain the mixture through a fine nylon sieve into a large jug, using the back of a ladle to press it through the sieve. Pour into six glasses and serve immediately.

HEALTHY TIP

If you don't want to use summer berries, you can replace them with iron- and fibre-rich apricots. Use either six ripe apricots, 16 ready-to-eat dried apricots or 400g (14oz) canned apricots in natural juice.

Serves 6, makes 900ml (1 ½ pints)

For the Slice – Ginger

1 **Grating** Peel a large section of the spice with a vegetable peeler and cut off any soft brown spots.
2 Using a wooden or fine metal grater resting on a small plate or bowl, grate the spice. Discard any large fibres adhering to the pulp.

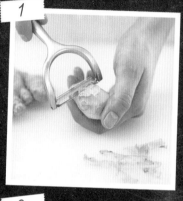

3 **Chopping** Cut slices off the spice
and cut off the skin carefully and
remove any soft brown spots. If
you need very large quantities,
you can peel a large section with a
vegetable peeler before slicing.

4 Stack the slices and cut into
shreds of the required thickness.
To make dice, stack the shreds
and cut to the required size.

5 **Pressing** If you need just the
juice, cut thick slices off the ginger
root and cut off the skin carefully,
taking care to remove any soft
brown spots under the skin. If
you need very large quantities,
you can peel a large section with
a vegetable peeler. Cut the slices
into chunks, and press them with a
garlic press into a small bowl.

4

Fruity Carrot with Ginger

TAKE 5

Hands-on time: 10 minutes

2 medium oranges

1cm (½in) piece fresh root ginger, peeled and roughly chopped

150ml (¼ pint) freshly pressed apple juice or 2 dessert apples, juiced

150ml (¼ pint) freshly pressed carrot juice or 3 medium carrots, 250g (9oz), juiced

mint leaves to decorate

1 Using a sharp knife, cut a slice of orange and put to one side for the decoration. Cut off the peel from the oranges, removing as much of the white pith as possible. Chop the flesh roughly, discarding any pips, and put into a blender. Add the ginger.

2 Pour in the apple and carrot juice and blend until smooth. Divide between two glasses, decorate with quartered orange slices and a mint leaf and serve.

HEALTHY TIP

This drink is full of vitamin C and betacarotene, an antioxidant that helps combat harmful free radicals and promotes healthy skin), making it a great immunity-boosting supplement. Fresh ginger is good for calming an upset stomach and providing relief from bloating and gas.

Serves 2, makes 600ml (1 pint)

Apple Crush

Hands-on time: 5 minutes, plus freezing

175g (6oz) strawberries
150ml (¼ pint) freshly pressed apple
   juice or 2 dessert apples, juiced
fresh strawberry leaves or fresh mint
   leaves to decorate

1 Remove the hulls from the
strawberries, then wash and pat the
fruit dry with kitchen paper. Put on
a tray and freeze for 40 minutes or
until firm.

2 When ready to serve, put the frozen
strawberries into a blender and pour
in the apple juice. Blend until smooth
and slushy. Pile into a serving glass
and decorate with strawberry or mint
leaves.

SAVE EFFORT

Try raspberries instead of
strawberries for a fruity variation
on this refreshing drink.

Serves 1, makes 300ml (½ pint)

Strawberry and Camomile Comforter

🍴 **Hands-on time:** 5 minutes, plus infusing and cooling

2 camomile teabags

5cm (2in) piece cinnamon stick

175g (6oz) strawberries

150ml (¼ pint) freshly pressed apple juice or 2 large dessert apples, juiced

1 Put the teabags and cinnamon stick into a small heatproof jug and pour in 150ml (¼ pint) boiling water. Leave to infuse for 5 minutes, then discard the bags and cinnamon stick. Leave to cool.

2 When ready to serve, remove the hulls from the strawberries, then wash and pat dry the fruit with kitchen paper. Put into a blender.

3 Pour in the apple juice and cold camomile tea and whiz for a few seconds until smooth. Pour into two tall glasses and serve.

SAVE EFFORT

Camomile teabags are very convenient and easy to use, but freshly dried camomile flowers will give a stronger flavour.

Serves 2, makes 600ml (1 pint)

327 cal ♥ 8g protein
15g fat (3g sat) ♥ 5g fibre
44g carb ♥ 0.1g salt

8

254 cal ♥ 6g protein
14g fat (2g sat) ♥ 3g fibre
29g carb ♥ 0g salt

10

279 cal ♥ 10g protein
6g fat (1g sat) ♥ 5g fibre
49g carb ♥ 0.2g salt

12

208 cal ♥ 7g protein
9g fat (trace sat) ♥ 3g fibre
28g carb ♥ 0g salt

16

187 cal ♥ 2g protein
1g fat (0g sat) ♥ 4g fibre
47g carb ♥ 0.1g salt

28

192 cal ♥ 3g protein
1g fat (trace sat) ♥ 3g fibre
45g carb ♥ 0.1g salt

30

300 cal ♥ 5g protein
19g fat (11g sat) ♥ 1g fib
29g carb ♥ 1g salt

34

393 cal ♥ 4g protein
23g fat (14g sat) ♥ 0.8g fibre
47g carb ♥ 0.7g salt

48

206 cal ♥ 9g protein
10g fat (6g sat) ♥ 1g fibre
20g carb ♥ 0.8g salt

52

180 cal ♥ 4g protein
6g fat (4g sat) ♥ 0.9g fibre
27g carb ♥ 0.1g salt

54

449 cal ♥ 21g protein
40g fat (19g sat) ♥ 0g fibre
1g carb ♥ 1g salt

66

835 cal ♥ 29g protein
79g fat (46g sat) ♥ 0g fibre
1g carb ♥ 2.8g salt

68

453 cal ♥ 22g protein
25g fat (6g sat) ♥ 3g fibre
38g carb ♥ 1.6g salt

70

440 cal ♥ 14g protein
36g fat (29g sat) ♥ 0.7g fibre
17g carb ♥ 1.8g salt

72

Calorie Gallery

193 cal ♥ 9g protein
8g fat (1g sat) ♥ 2g fibre
22g carb ♥ 0.3g salt

18

145 cal ♥ 11g protein
1g fat (0g sat) ♥ 5g fibre
30g carb ♥ 0.4g salt

20

188 cal ♥ 4g protein
7g fat (1g sat) ♥ 3g fibre
29g carb ♥ 0g salt

24

156 cal ♥ 1g protein
0g fat ♥ 2g fibre
40g carb ♥ 0g salt

26

376 cal ♥ 5g protein
25g fat (14g sat) ♥ 1g fibre
35g carb ♥ 0.7g salt

38

60 cal ♥ 2g protein
1g fat (0.1g sat) ♥ 0.5g fibre
12g carb ♥ 0.2g salt

40

140 cal ♥ 3g protein
5g fat (3g sat) ♥ 0.9g fibre
22g carb ♥ 0.7g salt

42

49 cal ♥ 0.8g protein
3g fat (0g sat) ♥ 0g fibre
6g carb ♥ 0.1g salt

44

137 cal ♥ 4g protein
1g fat (trace sat) ♥ 2g fibre
31g carb ♥ 0.3g salt

56

218 cal ♥ 5g protein
2g fat (trace sat) ♥ 2g fibre
49g carb ♥ 0.5g salt

58

333 cal ♥ 4g protein
22g fat (11g sat) ♥ 1g fibre
31g carb ♥ 0.5g salt

60

233 cal ♥ 4g protein
8g fat (5g sat) ♥ 0.8g fibre
38g carb ♥ 0.4g salt

62

457 cal ♥ 23g protein
34g fat (17g sat) ♥ 2g fibre
17g carb ♥ 2.7g salt

76

263 cal ♥ 19g protein
21g fat (8g sat) ♥ 2g fibre
1g carb ♥ 0.7g salt

78

238 cal ♥ 23g protein
21g fat (5g sat) ♥ 6g fibre
2g carb ♥ 0.6g salt

80

149 cal ♥ 12g protein
12g fat (3g sat) ♥ 1g fibre
0g carb ♥ 0.3g salt

82

174 cal ♥ 14g protein
12g fat (3g sat) ♥ 2g fibre
2g carb ♥ 0.2g salt

86

122 cal ♥ 7g protein
7g fat (1g sat) ♥ 2g fibre
9g carb ♥ 0.3g salt

88

290 cal ♥ 9g protein
13g fat (6g sat) ♥ 4g fibre
39g carb ♥ 0.6g salt

94

125 cal ♥ 3g protein
6g fat (3g sat) ♥ 0.5g fibre
17g carb ♥ 0.7g salt

96

259 cal ♥ 8g protein
20g fat (9g sat) ♥ 0.5g fibre
15g carb ♥ 0.7g salt

106

358 cal ♥ 8g protein
13g fat (7g sat) ♥ 0.5g fibre
54g carb ♥ 1.2g salt

108

175 cal ♥ 6g protein
4g fat (1g sat) ♥ 4g fibre
30g carb ♥ 0.5g salt

112

180 cal ♥ 5g protein
3g fat (1g sat) ♥ 1g fibre
34g carb ♥ 0.9g salt

114

429 cal ♥ 28g protein
20g fat (11g sat) ♥ 0.2g fibre
38g carb ♥ 3.1g salt

126

389 cal ♥ 17g protein
18g fat (10g sat) ♥ 2g fibre
41g carb ♥ 2.8g salt

128

384 cal ♥ 12g protein
31g fat (16g sat) ♥ 1g fibre
16g carb ♥ 1.9g salt

130

551 cal ♥ 32g protein
35g fat (22g sat) ♥ 1g fibre
27g carb ♥ 3.6g salt

132

172 cal ♥ 4g protein
1g fat (trace sat) ♥ 2g fibre
39g carb ♥ 0.2g salt

150

147 cal ♥ 5g protein
1g fat (trace sat) ♥ 8g fibre
39g carb ♥ 0.2g salt

152

133 cal ♥ 4g protein
1g fat (trace sat) ♥ 2g fibre
29g carb ♥ 0.2g salt

154

145 cal ♥ 6g protein
2g fat (1g sat) ♥ 3g fibre
27g carb ♥ 0.2g salt

158

141 cal ♥ 5g protein
5g fat (1g sat) ♥ 0.8g fibre
20g carb ♥ 0.1g salt

50 cal ♥ 2g protein
1g fat (9g sat) ♥ 0.3g fibre
9g carb ♥ 0.1g salt

392 cal ♥ 4g protein
16g fat (9g sat) ♥ 0.5g fibre
48g carb ♥ 0.7g salt

207 cal ♥ 6g protein
8g fat (4g sat) ♥ 1g fibre
31g carb ♥ 0.8g salt

284 cal ♥ 15g protein
14g fat (5g sat) ♥ 2g fibre
26g carb ♥ 0.9g salt

137 cal ♥ 14g protein
9g fat (5g sat) ♥ 3g fibre
5g carb ♥ 0.4g salt

364 cal ♥ 15g protein
9g fat (2g sat) ♥ 8g fibre
55g carb ♥ 2.1g salt

331 cal ♥ 26g protein
25g fat (4g sat) ♥ 0g fibre
38g carb ♥ 3.1g salt

246 cal ♥ 12g protein
9g fat (1g sat) ♥ 2g fibre
32g carb ♥ 0.4g salt

238 cal ♥ 16g protein
8g fat (1g sat) ♥ 2g fibre
25g carb ♥ 0.2g salt

205 cal ♥ 10g protein
3g fat (2g sat) ♥ 2g fibre
36g carb ♥ 0.3g salt

130 cal ♥ 9g protein
2g fat (1g sat) ♥ 1g fibre
24g carb ♥ 0.3g salt

108 cal ♥ 3g protein
1g fat (trace sat) ♥ 3g fibre
24g carb ♥ 0.1g salt

128 cal ♥ 2g protein
1g fat (trace sat) ♥ 5g fibre
30g carb ♥ 0.1g salt

100 cal ♥ 1g protein
trace fat ♥ 1g fibre
24g carb ♥ 0g salt

52 cal ♥ 1g protein
trace fat ♥ 1g fibre
13g carb ♥ 0g salt

Index

acidophilus 144
apple
  & almond yogurt 18–19
  & bran muffins 56–7
  compote 22–3
  crush 166–7
apricot orange smoothie 150–1
asparagus soldiers & egg 86–7

bagels, BLT-topped, & hollandaise sauce 130–1
banana
  creamy dairy-free 140–1
  & pecan muffins 52–3
vitality shake 138–9
beans, low-GI, on toast 122–3
bee pollen 148
berries 24–7, 58–9, 94–5, 152–5,
  168–9
    & toasted oats 8–9
  summer, smoothie 160–1
  blueberry
  & lemon pancakes 94–5
  muffins 58–9
bran & apple muffins 56–7
bread 112–17
  oatmeal soda 112–13
  orange eggy 108–9
  white farmhouse 114–15
brewer's yeast 144
brown sugar muffins 62–3
bruschetta, breakfast 20–1

camomile & strawberry comforter 168–9
carrot
  fruity, & ginger 164–5

spiced muffins 60–1
cinnamon
  pancakes 98–9
  whirls 44–5
compote
  apple 22–3
  strawberry 26–7
cranberry mango smoothie
  154–5
crêpes suzette 102–3
croissants 34–6
croque monsieur 132–3
crumpets 40–1, 128–9

Danish pastries 37–9

echinacea 144–5
egg 88–9, 126–7, 145
  baked 80–1
  boiled 85
  coddled 84
  duck, & asparagus 86–7
  eggs Benedict 72–3
  eggy orange bread 108–9
  omelettes 66–71
  poached 84
  poached, & mushrooms 78–9
  scrambled 74–5
  scrambled, & salmon 76–7
equipment 46–7

French toast 106–7
frittata, mixed mushroom 82–3
fruit pots, tropical 30–1
fruit salad, exotic 28–9

ginger 162–5
  fruity carrot & 164–5
ginseng 145
granola 10–11

haddock, smoked 68–9
  kedgeree 126–7
honey
  busy bee's comforter 148–9
  & spice loaf 48–9
  & yogurt muffins 54–5
huevos rancheros 88–9

kedgeree 126–7
kipper(s), traditional 124–5

lemon blueberry pancake 94–5
loaf, honey & spice 50–1

mango
  & cranberry smoothie 154–5
  & oat smoothie 158–9
  slicing 156
mozzarella mushrooms 120–1
muesli
  bars 14–15
  energy-boosting 16–17
muffins 50–1
  banana & pecan 48–9
  blueberry 58–9
  bran & apple 56–7
  brown sugar 62–3
  cheesy spinach 52–3
  honey & yogurt 54–5
  spiced carrot 60–1
mushroom
  & poached egg 78–9